Flute/Oboe
95C

ROBERT S. FROST
SACRED SETTINGS

CONTENTS

ISBN 0-8497-3360-X

Come, Thou Almighty King

Felice de Giardini
(1716-1796)

O Worship the King

Johann Michael Haydn
(1737-1806)

A Mighty Fortress

Martin Luther
(1483-1546)

The Doxology

Louis Bourgeois
(ca. 1510-1561)

O God, Our Help in Ages Past

William Croft
(1678-1727)

PRAYER OF THANKSGIVING

Netherlands Folk Song
(ca. 1625)

Come, Ye Thankful People, Come

George J. Elvey
(1816-1893)

FAITH OF OUR FATHERS

Henry F. Hemy
(1818-1888)

For the Beauty of the Earth

Conrad Kocher
(1786-1872)

Rock of Ages

Thomas Hastings
(1784-1872)

Now Thank We All Our God

Johann Crüger
(1598-1662)

Sweet Hour of Prayer

William B. Bradbury
(1816-1868)

Amazing Grace

from Walker's Southern Harmony
(1835)

Onward, Christian Soldiers

Arthur S. Sullivan
(1842-1900)

Nearer, My God, to Thee

Lowell Mason
(1792-1872)

Abide With Me

William H. Monk
(1823-1889)

Crusader's Hymn

Germany
(1842)

Lead, Kindly Light

John B. Dykes
(1823-1876)

The Heavens Resound

Ludwig van Beethoven
(1770-1827)

Fl. A
Fl. B
Ob. A
23
27
31
div.
rit.
*

Austrian Hymn

Franz Joseph Haydn
(1732-1809)

Christ the Lord is Risen

from Lyra Davidica
(1708)

AVE VERUM CORPUS

Wolfgang Amadeus Mozart
(1756-1791)

19
23
Fl. A
Fl. B
Ob. A
pp
27
mp
cresc. poco a poco
31
35
f
ff
39
p
pp
poco rit.

SOFTLY NOW THE LIGHT OF DAY

Carl Maria von Weber
(1786-1826)

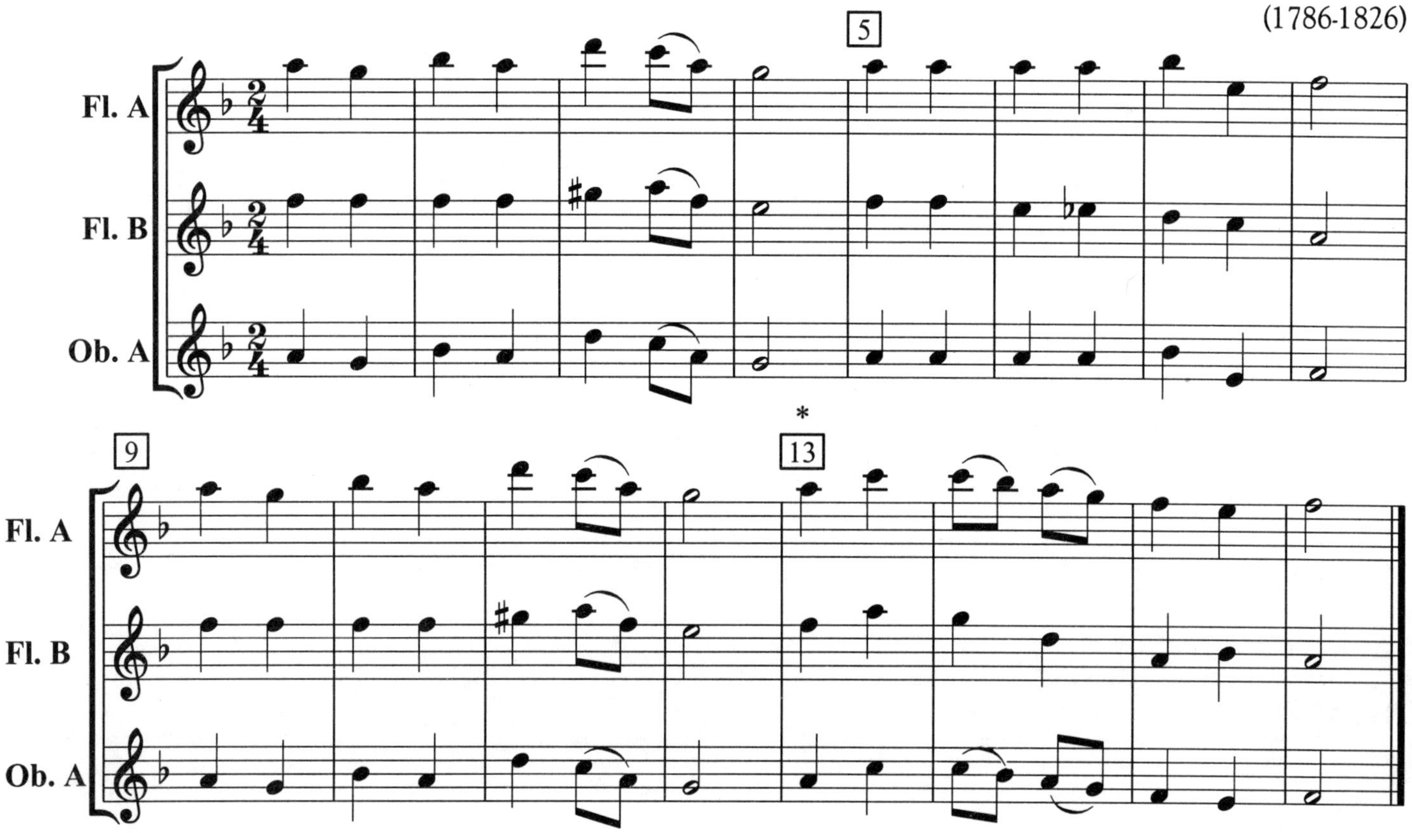

NOW THE DAY IS OVER

Joseph Barnby
(1838-1896)